How We Fell

HOW WE FELL

(a love story)

Glenn Colquhoun

illustrations by
Nikki Slade Robinson

STEELE ROBERTS
AOTEAROA NEW ZEALAND

ACKNOWLEDGEMENTS My gratitude to Chris Price and Vincent O'Sullivan for their advice with these poems and to Nikki Slade Robinson for her illustrations; she has been a joy to work with. Thanks also to Sarah Bolland, Lynn Peck, Laura Ranger and Matthew Bartlett for design and production work, and to Roger Whelan for his encouragement and help. My aroha as always to Roger Steele and Christine Roberts for continuing to put up with me along with my awkward collection of cats, dogs, seagulls, lists and tautologies.

National Library of New Zealand Cataloguing-in-Publication Data

Colquhoun, Glenn.
How we fell : a love story / Glenn Colquhoun ; illustrations by Nikki Slade Robinson.

ISBN 1-877338-91-5

I. Robinson, Nikki Slade. II. Title.
NZ821.2—dc 22

Printed by Astra Print, Wellington

STEELE ROBERTS
Box 9321, Wellington, Aotearoa New Zealand

info@steeleroberts.co.nz — www.steeleroberts.co.nz

for Barbara

… let this be held as resembling the truth.

Xenophanes

I didn't mean to fall in love when I did. I met somebody remarkable. For a while the sky was purple. There were twelve moons. When people talked their mouths moved so slowly you could see a man putting words between them as if he was keeping a scoreboard.

I didn't mean to fall out of love either. Ten years later I stared at the sky from flat on my back and wondered how I fell there.

The earth was soft. The tides were reliable. I wanted to tell her about it but I couldn't.

Every season since I pass each of these doorways at least once and remember living between them.

The contents

Let me describe for you her eyes

Her eyes were two guns
in the hands of a killer.
They drilled me before I
had a chance to drill them.

I did not even pick a fight

but lay there in the street before I knew it.

And the sun set blood-red.

And no one looked because they knew
they would get the same treatment.

And mothers called inside their obedient children.

Sheriffs crossed the road,
poking me with their sharp sticks,
complaining that they'd seen it all before
and of all the darn fool things…

Cars drove over me as if I wasn't there.

Cats licked me with their sandpaper tongues.

Doctors waited for the ambulance
and the ambulance waited for the police
and the police waited for the phone call

and the phone call never came.

Then she appeared at my side,

taking my head into her lap
and rocking at what she'd done,

timid as a small boy cleaning his gun,

wondering why the hell she went for hers,
wondering why the hell I went for mine.

That place
we met

I looked then
she looked then
I looked then
she looked then

I smiled then
she smiled then
I smiled then
she smiled then

I stopped then
she stopped then
I stopped then
she stopped then

I turned then
she turned then
I turned then
she was gone.

The arrangement of her skin

Some were responsible
for
the
bones
inside
her
neck

ladies
pouring
milk
into
the centre of their tea.

Some were responsible
for the construction
of her eyes

gaps in bars
where signs hung
warning people
NOT
to feed the lions.

Some were responsible
for the curve
of her shoulders

nurses folding sheets
around the corners
of their mattresses.

Some were responsible
for the muscle of
her thighs

rough sailors in tall
ships trimming their
fine sails taut

under moonlight.

What she first said

That Johnny Cash was the
greatest singer in the world

that his life had been tough
but he knew what it was like to live,

you could tell it from his face.

People called him The Man in Black.

The Man in Black. He was God.

That Kris Kristofferson wrote
the best songs ever written

and had the sexiest eyes,

you could tell he was kind
by looking at them.

People called him The Pilgrim.
"How's it going, Pilgrim?"

He reminded her of Jesus.

That Bette Midler was a great actress,
people called her The Divine Miss M

and Yeats was a great poet
but never got over the woman he loved
who did not love him.

That her brother's name was George.
He played soccer and all
the aboriginal boys liked him.

Manchester United was the greatest
soccer team in the world.
They had won the FA cup five times.

People called them The Red Devils.

"The Red Devils," I said.

"The Red Devils," she whispered.

"Go the Red Devils," we screamed.

The edge of the ledge we walked along with our arms outstretched

And so it began like rain,
with something
that was able to fall,

our skin as thin as water,
boiling up and moving
into the air like Christians
at the second coming.

Every cell was a bridegroom
taking off his belt
before bed,

every molecule an onion
cut into salads
with sharp knives,

every atom amok amongst sheep
…a mad dog finally
loosed off its chain…

collecting again into clouds

the shape of eyebrows,
the shape of stomachs,
the shape of smooth thighs.

And who is to say that my hand did not become hers,

or that her breath did not become mine,

or that that pale lump at the base of her throat
may not once have been my rib or
my nose or a word on the tip of my tongue.

We lived inside heaven,

with eagles and God and men
who had escaped from the law.

The world was the shape of a map.

We drew on its face,

stained it with coffee,

played noughts and crosses
on its thin black roads,

rolling it up and putting it away at last,

choosing not to look where it was
we had been before,

choosing not to look just
where it was we were going.

And how we fell

And how we fell and
how we fell and how
we fell and how we
fell and how we fell

And how we fell
fell

And how we fell
And how we fell
fell

And how we fell

And how we fell
And how we fell
And how we fell
And how we fell
And how we fell
And how we fell

And
how how
we we we
fell fell fell fell
and and and
how how
we

And how we fell
And how we fell
And how we
And how
And

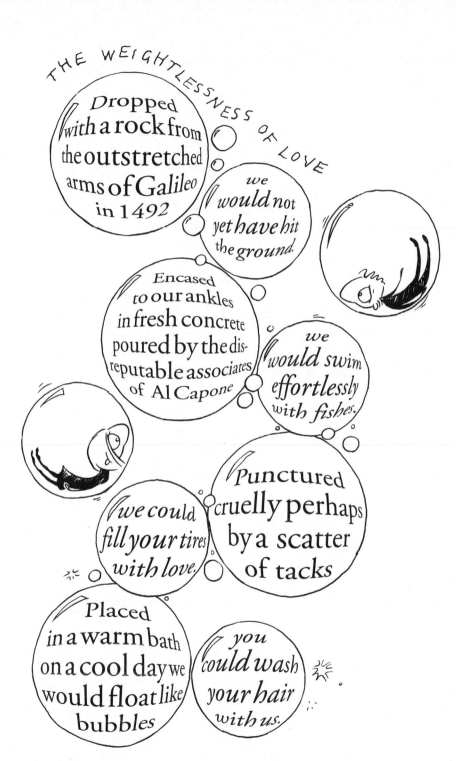

Dropped with a rock from the outstretched arms of Galileo in 1492

we would not yet have hit the ground.

Encased to our ankles in fresh concrete poured by the disreputable associates of Al Capone

we would swim effortlessly with fishes.

Punctured cruelly perhaps by a scatter of tacks

we could fill your tires with love.

Placed in a warm bath on a cool day we would float like bubbles

you could wash your hair with us.

19

What we saw on the way down

I.
God in heaven,
a bald spot spreading
like a stain on the
back of his head.

II.
Jesus working on his
motorcycle
in the back yard,
menacing as a teenager.

III.
The angels gathered silently
around a formica table,
watching Oprah on the TV.

IV.
The shapes of stars.
The tops of clouds.
The sides of mountains.

V.
The back of a large
black and white gull
searching for food.

VI.
The green earth lying back
on its sofa like a young man
watching cricket on the telly.

VII.
Those holes in mud
crabs scuttle to
when children pass.

VIII.
The sizzling flames of hell
burning six good priests
for auld lang syne.

IX.
Lucifer himself asking
all about our fall.

X.
But we did not see
anything at all.

Her accumulation from tiny drops of light

The porch lights of insomniacs at three in the morning shine along Central Avenue onto the Great South Road. At St George Street they cross north to Kolmar Road turning left, first left, left at the swimming pool, first right, through the lights and first right again after that.

This is the shape of her sleeping in bed.

Behind the bikesheds tough guys stand in semi-circles. They light cigarettes out of the wind. When sharp fires catch in the deep caves their hands make

her red lips crackle and burn.

From the safety of heaven, every Sunday, God looks down on the bright hats of good women sitting in church. Their fingers pick cotton from the hems of their skirts. When they bow their heads to pray, her eyelids flutter.

Her eyelids flutter.

Two red lights at a railway crossing in heavy rain blink together as if they were a quick dumb heart:

lub-dub
lub-dub
lub-dub
lub-dub

This is her smallest constellation.

Let me describe for you her lips

She kissed me first.

She will deny it
but she did.

I was there at the time

at least
in the beginning.

I was fresh kahawai
straight out of
the salt

shaken once or twice

then split
head to tail
into fine pieces
of white flesh

and placed

on her tongue
to melt like ice.

I was a frail child
wrapped securely
in blankets.

I was Satan
turned black in the
pyres of hell.

I was wine
swallowed straight
from the bottle

. . . .

. . . .

I do not know
what happened
after that…

That breeze of her upon the water

She was in the wind.

The storm at four o'clock in the
morning was her responsibility,

its powerful moan,
its sudden gusts,
its terrible expectations,

were nothing more than hers.

The shipwreck was all her doing

...safe,
...in harbour,
...on a fine day,
...against forecasts.

If you are looking for the spy who carried
the General's secrets across the field
on stealthy footsteps

then look no further than her.

She fanned the devil's fire.

She carried the good man's prayer.

She stole the policeman's whistle.
She took the bald man's hair.

She was behind the lover's letter
blown from his desk out the window,

down the street,
        over the trees,
                above the hedge,
        through the gate,
            around the corner,
                up the stairs

and into her bed.

When she arrives

the air pants like a horse
at the end of a race.

I step inside and bolt the door.

My chest fills out like an
old woman's dress.

Even the curtains begin to dance.

Ten summers and ten springs

After the beginning
there should be a middle.

All good stories have them:

the soldier returns to town and
tries to forget what he did,

families play happily inside
while the sky builds,

a burglar decides to go straight.

These are a less spectacular sun
perhaps, than the one rising
and the one setting,
but nonetheless capable of burning.

Ours was a old man's stomach:

the lawns were mowed,
visitors knocked on the door,
the rubbish was put out,
dishes were dropped on the floor.

Placed together end to end to end

they soon became that plain blue sea
love swam through like giant whales

migrating, until it appeared
the mundane corner of every wave
might be hiding
something magnificent.

About the beginning it must be said:

LADIES AND GENTLEMEN!
ON YOUR MARKS…
I NOW PRONOUNCE YOU…
LIGHTS, CAMERA, ACTION!!!

About the end it should be recorded:

THUNDER…HAIL…LIGHTNING!!
MAYDAY — MAYDAY — MAYDAY!!

But of the glorious middle,

ten summers and ten springs,

what should be said about
the bits in between?

Except, of course,
we did not know they were.

Let me describe for you her hands

Her fingers were ten strangers
who lived next door to each other.

The first was a small girl
wearing her mother's shoes.

The second was a whore who
wanted me to break the law.

The third was a boy in a denim shirt sitting
on his brother's motorbike in the back yard,
a thin line of black grease smiling
underneath his fingernails.

The fourth was as angry as sunset.

The fifth was worried the poor would starve,
that God would return when she wasn't looking,
that this time the car would not make the corner,
that someone would knock on her door.

The sixth had a mind bright with feathers.
It tore at her body with claws,
the way a bird trapped inside
scratches at its cage.

The seventh and eighth were twins.

One asked God every night for more faith.

One stole the offering from out of his plate.

The ninth was an old woman who had lived
long enough to get it right the next time.

The tenth was more beautiful
than a clear morning rising
after nine nights of silver rain.

The castle that we built

Down Tui Road we carried a brown lounge suite up a flight of stairs, over the balcony, through the windows, onto the floor, then sat on it like a summit. We had no flags. But the pub was noisy on a Friday night and Club Raro on Saturday. On Sunday we walked over broken glass. We promised each other that we would.

Near Preston Road I built a place to keep her clothes. They hung like a hedge with occasional flowers. Her skin was apple. The neighbour was mad. We painted the kitchen to keep it clean. Behind a fence the motorway barked like a dog.

At Redoubt Road we made love silently, scared of the walls and the people behind them. Tip-toeing along its secret paths we rested our bikes on the grass, climbed the fence, folded our clothes and held our breath. Throwing back our heads and laughing all the harder for the lack of noise we made, we listened to my sisters argue in the bathroom.

Along St George Street we hunted dragons, one by one from battlements we found at first unkempt. We filled the walls with noise, scrubbing the roof, sanding the doors, polishing the floors until they throbbed, sleeping while they creaked at night, every sound familiar, cramming them with details of ourselves and forever after that leaving them haunted.

Let me describe for you the dragons that we fought

Most came from respectable homes.

Their families were supportive.

On the whole, their childhoods
had been lived without
fear or traumatic incident.

It stood to reason they expected
a comfortable place to live,

the respect of neighbours,

a job they could be proud of

which meant at times tearing us
to pieces with their talons or

baking us black with their breath.

The stories they heard about us helped.

We were stupid,
unable to fly,
soft in the middle and bony.

In the end we had to admit
they were right.

They died like ripe fruit shaken
from the tree by bold neighbours,

the grass somehow covered in red plums.

We spat on the ground to get
their taste out of our mouths.

They always made us hungry.

Later, we stuck their heads on silver spikes
and hung their bones around our necks.

Although in our defence it should be said:
we came from respectable homes,

our lawns were neatly mowed,

our families did their best to be supportive,

and our childhoods were lived
for the most part
without fear or traumatic incident.

The dragon from the north

The dragon from the north
read books on how to be
a better dragon,

Leonardo on flying,
Dante on the smell of fire,
Revelation on how to persecute,

Shakespeare on getting the girl.

He practised for hours
in front of the mirror
his lumbering gait,

the flick of his tail the shape
of a perfect arrow.

Not brushing his teeth
after eating meat,
fingers and toes could
be clearly seen in his mouth
during polite conversation.

He was spectacular madness.
He was the dark storm howling,
He was the great ape with the girl in his hand.
He was the music rising to a climax.

He was as separate from safety
as it was possible to get,

something so easy to hate

we could not help but fall in love.

The dragon
from the south

The dragon
from the south was
half of me and half of her.

It only fought when
we were brought
together.

My arm.
Her leg.

My eyes.
Her neck.

Her lips.
My breath.

My heart.
Her chest.

My window looking over calm sea.
Her castle on the edge of a cliff.

My woman with her face to the door.
Her thief escaping the law.

My right.
Her left.

My east.
Her west.

Her laugh.
My cry.

Our roar.
Our sigh.

The dragon from the east

The dragon from the east
rode into war before the other
dogs could steal his food,

ten thousand men
on the backs of
ten thousand horses.

The world before him
was a bored bird turning.

The world after him:

death at its throat like
a young boy biting apples.

His axe split the heart
of a quiet soldier standing.

His sword took the neck of a king.

A spear stuck a spy
like a spike in the ribs,

his arrow, a Moor in the eye.

Twelve clean shots from the
barrels of his pearl-handled pistols
emptied into the bellies of six dumb
guards watching television.

Five later drowned in their soup.

One on the stairs was strangled with wire.

The guard dogs were poisoned with beef.

Waiting at the top of the stairs
the damsel, no longer in
distress, threw herself against
his chest like a medal.

He pressed his face lightly
into the curve of her neck.

Together they rode into a sunset
designed especially by those
who make calendars for a living.

Stopping at last by the railway
tracks on their way home he tied
her once more to the sleepers,

looking right then left
before slipping away,

preparing to gather an army.

The dragon from the west

The dragon from the west grew fat inside a seed,

counting out the petals, polishing the leaves, overseeing the insertion of its green shoots up and its green roots down. He insisted on spring and the widest possible bloom. He insisted on summer and the temperature of the sun. He insisted on winter and the thinness that came to be felt at the edge of each petal, preferring, at the final moment, to be rescued inside a grain of pollen by the last bee of autumn like a yellow helicopter.

Inside the bee the dragon soon had things running by clockwork.

He measured the bee and accounted for its depreciation: the decreasing property values, the falling outputs, the layings off, the arthritis. He was still balancing the books that day the old bee finally drove its sting into a spider. The dragon quickly fell inside a river.

The river walked to work in a pinstriped suit.

Later, it let its belt out notch by notch. After that it tore the seat out of its trousers, it wore a cardigan and pyjama pants, it shuffled to the fridge in its slippers. The dragon escaped in the last drop of water squeezed out of the river by the roots of a young tree clinging to its banks.

Under the guidance of the dragon the tree lived for five hundred years.

One day it lost a branch to a high wind. The second went when the people who lived behind it decided that they couldn't see the water. One struck a man on the head. After that the tree was never looked at the same way again. It feared the winter.

The dragon retired to the last branch of the old tree that was still turning green.

He entered the only apple or orange or pear that the tree could manage to bear. We saw its roundness at various times when we walked past and knew that it must be sweet. We knew that it would be easy. We thought that no one would notice. And so one day, without thinking, and without pausing, and because we were hungry, we took of the fruit and ate it.

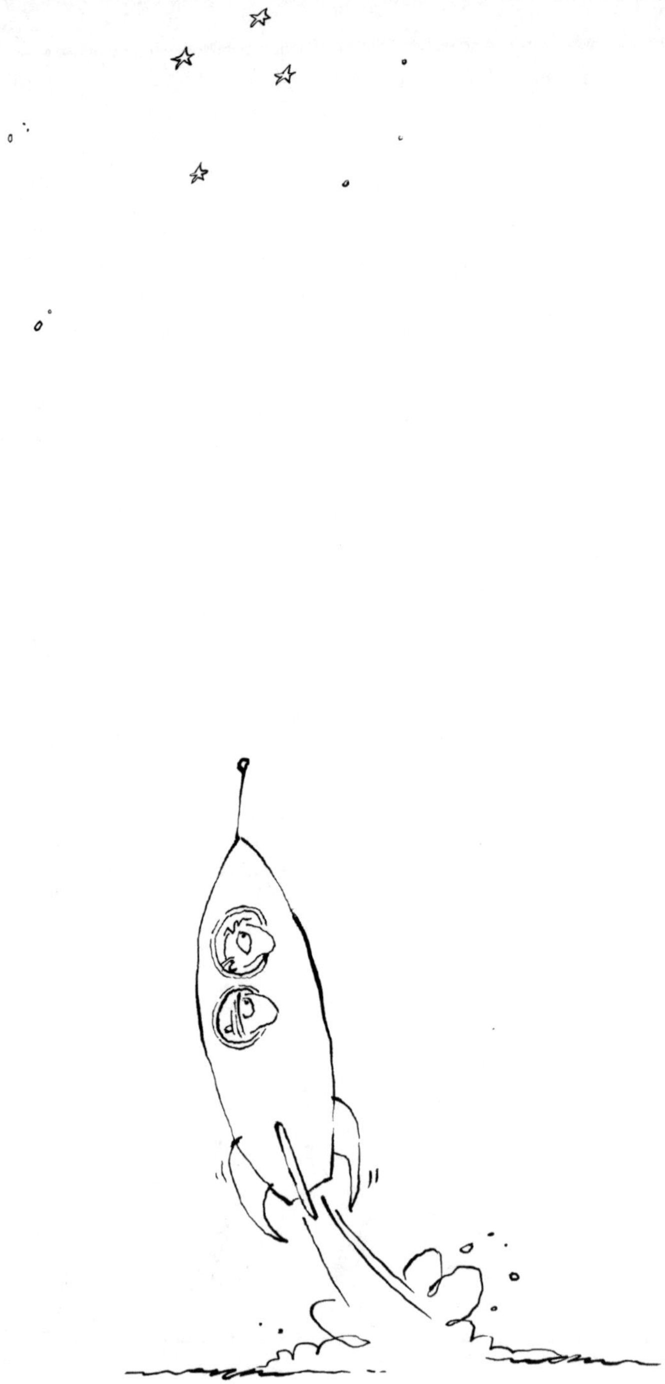

**Let me describe for you
the journeys that we took**

The moon was
covered in grey dust
and flowers,
it was hard to keep
our feet on
the ground.

The earth went
round and round.

Mars was too red,
we couldn't get
a drink anywhere.

The sun was too yellow,

we circled each
other instead.

The scorpion said
he knew a guy,
who knew a guy,

who knew a guy,
who'd break our legs.

At the hunter
and the hare,

we were too polite to stare.

When the archer
drew his bow,

we knew that it
was time to go.

We settled for
a sky as wide
as what she said
and I replied.

No one had ever been
there before.

THE JOURNEY OVER HIGH MOUNTAINS

During the day we climbed
During the night we rested
During the storms we howled
During the stillness, whispered

When it was warm we let go
When it was cold we held
Up every peak we were drawn
Down every valley we fell

Up every peak we whispered
Down every valley we howled
When it was warm we rested
When it was cold we yelled

During the day we struggled
During the night we held
During the storm we gathered
And during the stillness, fell

THE JOURNEY ACROSS DRY PLAINS

The journey across dry plains will always be remembered for the fact that despite never finding the water we were so desperately searching for it was all we ever thought about and touched and saw and drank

THE CROSSING OF DEEP WATER

She taught me how to swim. We talked about it in bed one night. I lay on the mattress and kicked my feet. She explained to me how the water would feel closing in around my skin. How it would be cold at first and then become warm. How it would be hollow at first and then become solid. I asked her what it was like underneath. She said that it was like having our skin completely exchanged for wet paint. I said it felt like melting and then I fell asleep, breathing in and out like the waves on a beach. She held me all night in her arms and when we woke up the next morning it felt like we were on the other side of something wide.

I taught her how to step on stones. I covered the bedroom floor with pillows and walked to the door without putting my feet on the carpet. She asked me what it was like on the other side. I talked about the grass and the streets and the buses. I said that the sky was open and closed at the same time. I said that it was noisy but that sometimes the sound was hard enough to stand on. I said that it was uncertain but at least we could rely on that. She reached out her hands and I held her all night in my arms. When we woke up the next morning it felt like we were on the other side of something wide.

45

Wednesday

✿ 31 · 2006

Thursday

1

The day before the day before yesterday:

I packed a warm coat and a good book.

She ate a square meal and asked the neighbour to feed her cat.

· ·

Friday

2

I locked my arms behind me

The day before yesterday: I checked the stove and barred the door.

She shut the windows and pulled the blinds.

Meeting 9:am

She closed her cautious eyes

· ·

Saturday

3

Yesterday:

We passed each other on our way.

I tipped my hat and said "Hello." She curtseyed and said "Good day."

· ·

Sunday

4

The rain will fall.

Today:

The sun will shine.

The wind will blow.

Meet for lunch!

The owl will call.

remember cat.

· ·

Monday

5

I will make a place beneath her eyes.

Tomorrow:

We will arrive. She will make a place between my arms.

Hairdresser 11:00 ▸ 11:45

· ·

Tuesday

6 *Buy shoes*

The next day:

We will rest.

She will not blink

And I will not let go.

APRIL

S	M	T	W	T	F	S
						1	2
4	5	6	7	8	9	10
11	12	13	14	15	16	17
18	19	20	21	22	23	24
25	26	27	28	29	30	

· ·

Wednesday

7

Meet 2:00 Pm

✳ Car WOF

JUNE

S	M	T	W	T	F	S
				1	2	3
6	7	8	9	10	11	12
13	14	15	16	17	18	19
20	21	22	23	24	25	26
27	28	29	30			

· ·

Thursday

8

And the day after the day after that:

Will be the day before the day before yesterday again.

· ·

Friday

Let me describe for you the sun of love

The sun of love was that memory
we all have of our father on
the best day of his life,

shirt off at the beach, teaching us to swim,

his back as rippled as God's footstep
left lightly on the
sand that day he drew us,

his arms, two lines of muscled hills
at either end of the universe,

his chest, two pillows smoothed gently
underneath the bedspread.

We would have kept him there forever

throwing stones, dodging waves,
kicking the ball as high as the moon into the sky,

riding on his back in front of all the other children,

turning wheelies after dark on the school lawn in the Monaro,

his voice as reassuring as the throb of engines on a plane,

that day when nothing could have been added to him,

or subtracted from him,

or shifted to his left,
or adjusted to his right,

or brought forward towards him,
or moved backwards away from him,

that would increase at all his volume,

that day we would not know was perfect until later,

by which time we might recognise the same small
sadness sitting fat inside all happiness...

asking if this is as good as it is possible to get

then what will be left for tomorrow?

Its belly full of bread

Love poked me
in the eye at first

hurt me in the
chest next

where it went
after that brought
no pain at all

although I ached.

Then it made
my belly
rise and fall.

I was not hungry
any more.

How autumn calls

Autumn calls
like an owl in the
middle of the night

More-pork

More-pork

More-pork

More-pork.

Autumn calls
like a dog barking
at a stranger round the
side of the house

Woof-woof

Woof-woof

Woof!
Woof!
Woof!
Woof!
Woof!

Autumn calls
like your favourite son
marching off to war

Left-right

Left-right

Left-right

Left-right

Autumn calls
like your phone nagging
when you are sitting
down to dinner

Ring-ring

Ring-ring

Ring-ring

Ring-ring

sure it will be
for someone else.

That final morning before the storm

It was as though we were
asleep and I woke first.

I watched the sun rise.

I remember it was yellow
with blue eyes.

The combination was striking.

It was rolling out the sky but
a bit had got stuck in one corner
like a piece of lettuce between its teeth.

I said it was like that lettuce.

I thought we were getting on well.

I said I didn't want any trouble.

The sun grunted and licked
at its gums with its tongue.

She was right beside me then like
tomorrow or breathing or sin,

something no one would notice
until it was gone and then
they could not live without it.

The forecast was for sunshine and clear skies.

It was the one they used for weddings
and for picnics and for
cricket and for the *Titanic*.

We should have known that it would rain.

At the first drop we took in the washing.

The wind we did not particularly like
but we had seen it all before.

When the thunder clapped we decided
we were in a storm but
did not take it personally.

When the water rose we agreed to call it a flood.
We stood in our doorways until we
remembered that that was just for earthquakes.

She waited for me on the stairs.

But when I turned around
I found she was not there.

No fond farewells.
No music rising.
No knock at the door.

No metaphors except for
words themselves.

The panic was panic.
The fear was fear.
The loss was loss or at least
what it was before we called it that.

The emptiness was endless and wide
but always the distance between
my stomach and my throat.

And into it the wind continued to blow
and the rain continued to pour.

I could not find her after that.

Perhaps she went next door.

Perhaps I will be back in a minute.

My heart was a fish
in a boat
gasping for air,

which was strange because all
around me the wind was howling.

The edge of the ledge we walked along with our arms outstretched

In the beginning our path was broad and wide, like that one in the Bible the damned walk on during their journey to destruction.

I cannot remember when it became narrow, the width of a river. We shaded our eyes with our hands to see the other side.

How we got from there to balancing on the brick wall outside our house I do not know, our arms outstretched, crocodiles swimming through the grass in case we fell. I thought we were pretending until we looked down.

And found ourselves on the razor's edge, our feet so bloody that for certain periods of time we had to carry each other on our backs, pretending that it did not hurt, ready to move on again until I said "You go first" and she said "You go first" and I said "You go first" and she said "You go first"...

And how we fell

Our kisses
we sent
to the Devil.

Our cuddles
we gave
to the poor.

Our hearts
we sold
to the butcher.

He gave us a
silver coin.

We bought
a pair
of pistols.

We bought
the crack
of dawn.

We bought
a pair of
solid boots.

And off
we marched
to war.

Let me describe for you the death of love

Our love died like a bad actor on stage, with a loud *aaarrrggghhhh!!!* Shot twice in the chest, he staggered to a window, breaking it in slow motion, before falling head first from a tall building onto the roof of a passing car.

Pulling himself slowly to his feet, he held onto the metal flagpole which had skewered him on the way down, while his trousers burst into flame from the cigarette butt tossed casually from a window by a passing motorist.

His cries echoed through the street for the kilometre he limped to the wharves, where he was beaten by local thugs and cast into the sea. Washing up with the tide, he pirouetted on one foot, then the next, until he stumbled onto the railway tracks, where he failed to notice the 12:30am train speeding towards him.

Later, after being backed over by the ambulance, he woke tethered to a row of monitors in the Intensive Care Unit, only to be told he had inoperable lung cancer, almost certainly caused by passive smoking in the workplace, with only a one point four percent five-year survival rate; at which point he lapsed into a coma when one of the doctors stumbled over an extension lead.

His heart continued to beat on screen while a young nurse watched, waiting for the next exciting episode. The one where the earthquake arrives followed by the flood, volcanic eruption, devastating killer virus and crazed psychotic clown until eventually the show was scrapped and the scriptwriters died their appropriate deaths and Charlton Heston found the Statue of Liberty half-buried on a deserted beach. At which time the nurse woke from sleeping next to her patient's chest, convinced she felt at last a definite albeit weak tug pulling against the palm of her hand.

The particular indifference of the sea

The tide was out
when I met her.

It was out the first
time we kissed.

It was in when we
bought the couch.

It lapped at our bed
when we touched

*the burglar moon
with his torch in
the window heaving*

but still it would
not budge.

It was out when
we climbed to Heaven.

It was in when
we took the bus.

It was there when
I saw her last

*packed into boxes
by the intersecting
frames of the
kitchen window.*

It is hard to believe
it does not care.

That winter of our discontent

Sorrow is a type of sea

with tides and waves
and creatures to take you
in their jaws and squeeze.

It enters the heart.

It enters through the
red door of the chest.

It floods the throat.

It fills the lungs.
It fills the lungs until it breathes.

It approaches the limbs.

It approaches the limbs
like a young man riding his bike
through the English countryside.

It takes the hands.
It takes the feet.

It takes the toes which
struggle briefly
for a last touch of the sand.

The body is a pale boat.

The body is the roof
of a house in flood.

On it float the television, the radio,
a cat and dog,
your sons and daughters,

all that might be rescued;

a wet man perhaps,

sitting with his arms held
tightly around his knees.

What time would tell

There was a time
when the gap
between us
was so narrow
I could have stretched out my fingers towards her in the dark
and closed it.

It would have been the span of my hand at most

fingertip to thumb;

a hesitation.

Even a glance would
have secured us.

I could have
screwed it up then
like a piece of paper
and thrown
it into the bin

but I didn't.

In time it was the width of the couch.

She looked
across at
me and laughed

calling *Jump*,
then *Jump*,

then *Jump*.

At last it occupied
the emptiness
of an entire room.

I stared at the hole between us and thought it simpler to carry on around
the world until
I reached
the other side.

I feel sure I will arrive
one day soon.

The solitude of flight

Down
and
down
and
down

I plunged

past the Father
past the Son.

Said the
bishop,

to the nun

I can't undo
what
he has
done.

Down
and
down
and
down

I fell

past the steeple
past the bell

down to where
the Devil
dwelt

not
even
he
knew
how
I felt.

THOSE THINGS WE MIGHT HAVE SAID OVER WAR

How mourners clean
the field after battle

...I said he was going to crack...
...too much pressure...

...didn't have the temperament...

...finishing was poor...

...placed on the rack...
...something had to give...

...she was always going to struggle...

...out of her depth...
...never in it...
...all over the place...

...she dropped her bundle...

...it wouldn't have happened in my day...

...it was the bounce of the ball...
...it was the referee...

...it was the luck of the draw...

...it was the wind...
...it was the crowd...
...it was the scoreboard...

...it was the toss of the coin...

...a breakdown in communication...
...conditions had a lot to do with it...

...it's not the last we'll hear of it...

...one thing's for certain...

...there wasn't any love lost
   out there today...

The life of the wound

The wound was clean at first,
the shape of me in her,
the shape of her in me,
two lips before make-up,
so cool I wanted to light a cigarette.

Soon it was the talk of the town.
Everyone wanted to meet it.
Old people poked it.
Children threw stones.
The *Woman's Weekly* wrote a series of in-depth articles.

Years passed and the wound put on weight.
It examined itself in mirrors and wondered if it was losing its looks.
One day someone threw a chip packet inside,
then a newspaper, then a shopping trolley.
Eventually, it was rumoured, a body was found,
wrapped securely in a series of cheap plastic rubbish bags.

Somebody made a movie about mobsters
and people moved back into the area.
They did up houses, built cafés, sold expensive clothes
and found the wound cool. The wound practised looking
deeper than it was. Later, the market crashed.
Everyone seemed to have enough wounds of their own.

The wound moved out of the city and
bought a cottage beside the water.
It thought about tying things up at last.
It considered a row of buttons or some stitches or a zip.
When the time seemed right it went outside
with a shovel and started to dig.

It filled in its right side but its left side opened up.
It filled in its left side but its right side gaped.
Each time it grew smaller it enlarged.
Each time it filled up it emptied.

At which point the wound stopped trying to pull itself together,
saw again the shape of her and the shape of me
and the shape of two lips before make-up
and in that moment once more remembered
the exquisite pressure of kissing.

That place inside me
where she was

It is possible to say,

now:

she was my holy day,

that day my city was built,

that morning I robbed the
natives blind and

threw a generation of
my finest to death
for a ridiculous war.

She was that day
I walked with Jesus
through the streets
and knocked him

blow by blow

into the wood.

In time to come,

when men walk over me,
tending sheep,

they might kick
with luck
an empty bottle or two,

a shard of pottery

and laugh at what we thought
would hold water forever.

Be sure of one thing,

I loved her.

When all else falls
let this be the one small
vessel a goatherd
lifts out of the sand.

She was my time.

There was no
before
before her,

and afterwards
can now
only ever be

afterwards.

I used to think
I would not die.

Now I know otherwise.

Let me describe for you the quality of scars

Some years from now they will discover our scars.

The first will be found at the bottom of an excavation searching for gold. There will be an announcement on the television. There will be controversy on the radio. There will be those who believe that it should be left in the ground where it was found. There will be those who believe that it should be loaded onto a truck and placed in a museum. Most will not care, turning the page to see where the sales can be found on Saturday or changing the channel to discover which woman left with only a bikini and a camera crew will survive the longest on a desert island.

The second scar will be found in the night sky. It will be seen at first through a telescope aligned precisely at the right time, at the right place, on the right angle. An astronomer will shout "There, there, there" until everyone can see it, a constellation the shape of a smile or the shape of a frown or the shape of a woman curled around the hollow of a man who has left her. Some will argue that it is new and forget how old it is. Some will recognise it for what it is and walk away. Some will wonder if it could somehow sustain life and forget what life it has sustained. Missionaries will rub their hands together. They will give it a name when it already has one.

The last scar will be found on the heart itself, fine enough to be seen only under the gaze of the most powerful microscope. To the naked eye it will appear to be a thin line, equivalent to the boundary between two sheets of red wallpaper. On the tenth power it will approximate the stitches sewn in a clean wound to keep it from gaping. On the hundredth power it will look like the outstretched arms of sailors passing frantic women and children onto a lifeboat from a sinking liner, the sound of water splashing as the odd one slips between. On the ten thousandth power a young man writes I LOVE YOU in huge letters on a wild beach, finding it more and more difficult to get to the end of his sentence before the waves wash away its beginning.

The ambush of memory

Some time ago I bumped into her.

She was crouched like a Japanese
soldier living in a cave
on a forgotten Pacific atoll.

I said, "What the hell are you doing here?"
She aimed her gun at me and
shouted not to move.

I said, "The war is over, it finished years ago.
I remember signing the papers."

She said, "Whore-of-Satan!"

I said, "Couldn't we just talk about it?"
She said, "Death-to-the-enemy."

I said, "I thought you already knew."
She drew her sword and CHAAARRRRGED!

We fought hand-to-hand for a while, lunging
clumsily with bayonets, then sticks, then
with our bare hands at each other's throats,

fingers in eyes, up noses, biting,
kicking, scratching, pulling hair,

tasting her breath, smelling her sweat,
listening to her heaving chest

…rising…falling…

…my face pressed into her
…her face pressed into me.

It was just like the old days.

She said, "What do we do now?"
I said, "I don't know."

She said, "Sorry about the language."
I said, "It was to be expected."

She said, "Do you remember?"
I said, "How could I forget."

Love slid its knife into me so
kindly then it made me cry.

My heart became stooped in an instant.

Which was unusual because
no matter how many times
I saw her after that, she never
seemed to look any older.

The forgiveness of love

I do not want
to write of love:
it is a ripe apple
on a full tree.

I want to write:
it is that thin worm crawling towards me.

I do not want
to write of love:
it is that thin worm crawling towards me.

I want to write:
it is an owl
with a quick
beak, staring.

I do not want
to write of love:
it is an owl
with a quick
beak, staring.

I want to write:
it is a cat
about to sink
its claws
into a bird.

I do not want
to write of love:
it is a cat
about to sink
its claws
into a bird.

I want to write
that love
is a wild dog
barking.

The immediate distance

Today is another day, a day
much the same as any other day.

Similar to the one before it.
Similar to the one behind it.

Similar to the one on its right.
Similar to the one on its left.

Similar to the one above it.
Similar to the one below.

Similar, similar, similar, similar.

It will begin with sunrise,

sleep being rubbed from my eyes,
milk being checked in the fridge,
too much butter on the toast.

It will progress to noon,

the sky in shorts and T-shirt
kicking a ball through a yard.

From there it will turn into evening,

ten thousand streetlights burning
sharply through the night.

But it will still be another day without her,

to be placed in a pile reserved
for all days spent without her,

a small mountain of empty shells
growing steadily in one corner of my life
until that time where they balance exactly
those days that were spent beside her.

At that point my joy will be equal to my sorrow,

my wrong will be equal to my right,

what was lost will be equal to what was found.

And at that point we might somehow be
free to meet one day at the shops with
nothing to remember and nothing to forget,

discussing the library books we were returning,
leaving each other charmed, beguiled, delighted,
wondering if we might somehow
meet in someone else again.

But I suspect that day will never come
and that this mountain will grow for two
or three more lifetimes yet, until

from its very top I can look down
like a bird on what we did together and
only then believe that it is finished.

Let me describe for you her eyes

Her eyes were two guns
in the hands of a killer.
They drilled me before I
had a chance to drill them.

I did not even pick a fight

but lay there in the street before I knew it.

And the sun set blood-red.

And no one looked because they knew
they would get the same treatment.

And mothers called inside their obedient children.

Sheriffs crossed the road,
poking me with their sharp sticks,
complaining that they'd seen it all before
and of all the darn fool things…

Cars drove over me as if I wasn't there.

Cats licked me with their sandpaper tongues.

Doctors waited for the ambulance
and the ambulance waited for the police
and the police waited for the phone call

and the phone call never came.

Then she appeared at my side,

taking my head into her lap
and rocking at what she'd done,

timid as a small boy cleaning his gun,

wondering why the hell she went for hers,
wondering why the hell I went for mine.